Introduction to OpenCV 3

Application Development for Ultimate Beginners

Table of Contents

Introduction

Most computer software applications today are expected to have vision capabilities. Implementation of such a feature in any software application is easy by use of the OpenCV library. This is a computer vision library which can be used for implementation of vision features in software applications. The good thing about the library is that it is compatible with a number of programming languages including C, C++, Java, and Python. These are the common programming languages which are widely used in the development of computer software applications. This explains why you should learn how to use this library. This book guides you on how to use this library in C++, Java, and Python. Most of the features of OpenCV are

Chapter 1- What is OpenCV?

Open Computer Vision Library (OpenCV) is an open source computer library with vision capabilities. It is also used in machine learning and image processing. The library now has GPU acceleration which can be used for real-time operations. The library was released under the BSD license, making it available for free for both academic and commercial purposes. It comes with interfaces for C, C++, Java, and Python and it can be used on the Windows, Linux and Mac OS, Android, and the iOS operating systems.

The OpenCV library was solely developed for computation efficiency and to be used for the processing of real-time operations. The library was written optimized for C/C++ and one can use it for multi-core processing.

Applications of OpenCV

The OpenCV library can be applied in following fields:
- Automated surveillance and inspection
- Image/video search and retrieval
- Robot navigation and control
- Movies- 3D structure from motion
- Street view image stitching
- Interactive art installations
- Medical image analysis

Setting up an OpenCV Environment

For you to setup the OpenCV environment in your computer, you must first download it. You can download it from **http://opencv.org/**. In this book, we will be discussing OpenCV 3.3 which is currently the latest version of OpenCV, so download it.

A file with .exe extension will be downloaded to your system, so go ahead and extract it so as to create a folder on your system. Navigate through OpenCV → build → java and you will find a .jar file. Save the file in some other folder to be used further.

We will be showing you how to install OpenCV to be used for Java.

Once you have downloaded the jar files, they should be embedded in your eclipse environment. This can be done by building the path to the JAR files by the use of pom.xml.

Setting the Build Path

The following steps will help you to setup OpenCV in your Eclipse environment:

1. First, ensure that you have Eclipse installed in your system. If not, just download it and then install it on your computer.

2. After the installation completes, launch Eclipse, then click File, New, and then Open.

3. Click Project and the window for creating a new project will be opened. Choose a Java Project, and then proceed by clicking on Next.

4. Right click the new project which has been created, and then choose "Build Path." Click on "Configure Build Path..."

5. Once you have clicked on "Build Path," you will be taken to the wizard for Build path. Click on the "Add External JARs" button. Navigate to the path where you saved your .jar file.

6. Click the Open button, and the files will be added to your library. Once you have clicked OK, the required JAR files will be added to your current project and you will be able to verify the added files simply by expanding Referenced Libraries.

Setting a Path for Native Libraries

Other than the Jar files, you should also set the path for the Native libraries, that is, the DLL files, for OpenCV. To find the DLL (dynamic link libraries), open the installation folder for OpenCV and then open the build->java subfolder. You will find that both the 64 bit and 32 bit folders have the dll libraries for OpenCV.

Open the right folder based on the operating system you are using and you will see the dll file. Again, open the window for JavaBuildPath. You will see the JAR file which has been added as well as the JRE System Library. The path for the file can be set by following the steps given below:

1. Launch the JavaBuildPath window. You will see the JAR file which has been added, as well as the JRE System Library.

2. Expand it and you will see the system libraries as well as the location of the Native library location.

3. Double click the Native library location and you will see the window for "Native Library Folder Configuration."

4. Click the External Folder... button, and then choose the location of the dll file in your system.

Installation on Linux

For you to install OpenCV on Linux, you should have the following packages installed on your system:

- GCC 4.4.x or a later version

- Git

- CMake 2.6 or a higher version

- GTK+2.x or a higher version, including headers (libgtk2.0-dev)

- Python 2.6 or a later version and Numpy 1.5 or a later version with developer packages (python-numpy, python-dev)

- pkg-config

- ffmpeg or libav development packages: libavformat-dev, libavcodec-dev, libswscale-dev

- [optional] libdc1394 2.x

- [optional] libtbb2 libtbb-dev

- [optional] libjpeg-dev, libtiff-dev, libpng-dev, libjasper-dev, libdc1394-22-dev

The following commands can help you install the packages:

sudo apt-get install build-essential

sudo apt-get install cmake git libgtk2.0-dev pkg-config libavcodec-dev libavformat-dev libswscale-dev

sudo apt-get install python-dev python-numpy libtbb2 libtbb-dev libjpeg-dev libpng-dev libtiff-dev libjasper-dev libdc1394-22-dev

After that, visit sourceforge, and then download the source code for the latest version of OpenCV. After downloading the tarball, unpack it.

You can use CMake to build the OpenCV from source from the command line. The following steps are necessary:

1. Create a temporary directory, where you will keep the files which are generated, the project files, the object files, and the output binaries. We will denote this as <cmake_binary_dir>.

2. Enter <cmake_binary_dir> and then type the following:

   cmake [<some optional parameters>] <path to the OpenCV source directory>

   Consider the following example:

cd ~/opencv
mkdir release
cd release

cmake -D CMAKE_BUILD_TYPE=RELEASE -D CMAKE_INSTALL_PREFIX=/usr/local ..

3. Enter the temporary directory which you have created, that is, <cmake_binary_dir>, and then proceed with the following:

   make
   sudo make install

Chapter 2- Storing Images

We use devices like scanners and cameras for the purpose of capturing images. The devices usually record the numerical or the pixel values of the image. The OpenCV library will in turn process the digital images, and there is a need for the images to be stored for processing.

The OpenCV library comes with a class known as "Mat" which can be used for the purpose of storing the values of an image. The image values are stored in the form of an n-dimensional array. The class is used for storing image data of color or grayscale images, vector fields, voxel volumes, tensors, point clouds, histograms etc.

The class has two data parts, the header and the pointer. These are described below:

1. Header- this stores information such as size, storage method and address of the matrix, which is constant in size.

2. Pointer- for storing pixel values of an image, and this keeps on changing.

In the OpenCV Java library, this class is used with the same name (Mat) and it can be accessed from the org.opencv.core package.

The class comes with multiple constructors which can be used for construction of the Mat object. Let us discuss some of these constructors:

1. Mat()
   This is the default construct and it has no parameters by default. It is used for creating an empty matrix which is then passed to other OpenCV methods.

2. Mat(int rows, int cols, int type)

This constructor takes three integer arguments which represent the number of rows and columns in 2D array as well as the type of the array.

3. Mat(int rows, int cols, int type, Scalar s)
   This constructor has additional parameter, and it is capable of accepting objects of the class Scalar as a parameter.

4. Mat(Size size, int type)
   This constructor accepts only two parameters, one for matrix size and the other for specifying the type of array for storing the data.

5. Mat(Mat m, Range rowRange)
   This constructor will accept an object of some other matrix as well as an object of class Range representing the rows which will be used for creating the matrix.

6. Mat(Mat m, Rect roi)
   This constructor will accept two objects, one to represent the other matrix and the other to represent the Region Of Interest.

How to Create and Display a Matrix

In this section, we will be guiding you on how to create and display a simple OpenCV matrix. The following are the necessary steps for you to do this:

Load OpenCV Native Library

When using the OpenCV library to write Java code, you can use the loadLibrary() function so as to load the OpenCV native library. The following statement can help you load the library:

**System.loadLibrary
(Core.NATIVE_LIBRARY_NAME);**

Instantiating the Mat class

There are various functions which can be used for this purpose. The following statement can be used for this purpose:

```
//Creating a matrix
Mat matrix = new Mat(5, 5, CvType.CV_8UC1, new Scalar(0));
```

Filling the Matrix

To retrieve specific rows/columns of a matrix, you have to pass the index values to the rows() and cols() methods. The values to these can be set by use of the variants of setTo() methods. This is shown below:

```
//Retrieving a row with index 0
Mat row0 = matrix.row(0);

//setting values of the elements in the row with an index of 0
row0.setTo(new Scalar(1));

//Retrieving row with index 3
Mat col3 = matrix.col(3);

//setting the values of all the elements in row with index 3
col3.setTo(new Scalar(3));
```

The following code can help you to create a simple matrix in Java and display it by use of the OpenCV library:

```
import org.opencv.core.Core;
import org.opencv.core.CvType;
import org.opencv.core.Mat;
import org.opencv.core.Scalar;

class DisplayingMatrix {
```

```java
public static void main(String[] args) {
    //Load the core library

System.loadLibrary(Core.NATIVE_LIBRARY_NAME);

    //Create the matrix
    Mat matrix = new Mat(5, 5, CvType.CV_8UC1, new Scalar(0));

    //Retrieve the row at index 0
    Mat row0 = matrix.row(0);

    //set the values of all the elements in the row at index 0
    row0.setTo(new Scalar(1));

    //Retrieve the row at index 3
    Mat col3 = matrix.col(3);

    //set the values of all the elements in the row at index 3
    col3.setTo(new Scalar(3));

    //Print the matrix

    System.out.println("The OpenCV Mat data:\n" + matrix.dump());
    }
}
```

The JavaSE API

The class BufferedImage provided in the java.awt.image.BufferedImage is used for image storage, while the ImageIO class provided in the "import javax.imageio" package comes with methods for reading and writing to the images.

The following Java code can help you to load and save images by use of the JavaSE library:

```
import java.io.File;
import java.io.IOException;
import java.awt.image.BufferedImage;
import javax.imageio.ImageIO;

public class LoadingImage_JSE_library {
  public static void main( String[] args ) throws IOException {
    //Input the File
    File input = new File("C:/EXAMPLES/OpenCV/sample.jpg");

    //Read the image
    BufferedImage image = ImageIO.read(input);

    //Save the image using a different name
    File ouptut = new File("C:/OpenCV/image1.jpg");
    ImageIO.write(image, "jpg", ouptut);

    System.out.println("Image has been Saved");
  }
}
```

You can navigate to the path which is specified in the code, and you will find that the image has been saved.

Chapter 3- Reading Images

The ImageCodes class which is provided by the org.opencv.imgcodecs package comes with methods for reading and writing images. With OpenCV, it is possible for you to read an image and then store it in a particular matrix. Transformations can be carried out on the matrix if there is a need. The processed matrix can later be written to a file.

The ImageCodes class provides the read() method which can be used for reading images with OpenCV. The method takes the following syntax:

imread(filename)

The argument "filename" is of string type, and it specifies the path to the image which is to be read.

Let us discuss the steps which are necessary for one to read an image in OpenCV:

Use the "load()" method so as to load the image:

System.loadLibrary(Core.NATIVE_LIBRARY_NAME);

Next, create an instance of the ImageCodecs class as shown below:

Imgcodecs imageCodecs = new Imgcodecs();

Next, you can use the imread() method so as to read the image. The method accepts only a string variable which is the path to where the image to be read is located, and the read image is returned as a Mat object. This method can be used as follows:

Mat matrix = imageCodecs.imread(Path to the image);

The following is a full code which shows how one can read a full image in Java using OpenCV:

```java
import org.opencv.core.Core;
import org.opencv.imgcodecs.Imgcodecs;
import org.opencv.core.Mat;

public class ReadingImages {
  public static void main(String args[]) {
    //Load the OpenCV core library
    System.loadLibrary(
Core.NATIVE_LIBRARY_NAME );

    //Instantiate the Imagecodecs class
    Imgcodecs imageCodecs = new Imgcodecs();

    //Read the Image from file
    String file ="C:/USERS/OpenCV/image1.jpg";
    Mat matrix = imageCodecs.imread(file);

    System.out.println("Image has been Loaded");
  }
}
```

Once you run the program, the OpenCV will load the image specified and the message "Image has been Loaded" will be displayed.

Reading Images in C++

That is how you can read a file using Java code and OpenCV. What about in C++? For you to do this, you must first install OpenCV and then integrate it with Visual Studio. This should involve adding the OpenCV libraries as dependencies to your project. You can then write the following code:

```cpp
#include "opencv2/highgui/highgui.hpp"
#include <iostream>
```

```cpp
using namespace cv;
using namespace std;

int main( int argc, const char** argv )
{
    Mat img = imread("Pic1.JPG",
CV_LOAD_IMAGE_UNCHANGED); //read the image
data contained in the file "Pic1.JPG" then store it in
'img'

    if (img.empty()) //check whether your image has
been loaded or not

    {
        cout << "Error : Image cann't be loaded" <<
endl;
        //system("pause"); //wait for key press
        return -1;
    }

    namedWindow("MyWindow",
CV_WINDOW_AUTOSIZE);
//create a window with name "MyWindow"

    imshow("MyWindow", img); //display the image
stored in the 'img' in "MyWindow" window

    waitKey(0); //wait for infinite time for keypress

    destroyWindow("MyWindow"); //destroy window
named, "MyWindow"

    return 0;
}
```

Before you can run the program, ensure that you have an image named Pic1.JPG where you have the C++ file. You will see the image loaded in a window.

Chapter 4- Writing Images

The ImageCodes class comes with the write() method which can help us write images by use of OpenCV. The process has to first follow the first three steps discussed in the previous chapter. You should then invoke the method inwrite() of the ImageCodecs class so as to write the image. The method takes the syntax given below:

imwrite(filename, mat)

The "filename" is a string parameter which specifies the path in which we want to save the file. The second parameter, mat, is a Mat object which specifies the image which is to be written.

The following are the necessary steps for you to write an image in Java using OpenCV:

Use the "load()" method so as to load the image:

System.loadLibrary(Core.NATIVE_LIBRARY_NAME);

Next, create an instance of the ImageCodecs class as shown below:

Imgcodecs imageCodecs = new Imgcodecs();

Next, you can use the imread() method so as to read the image. The method accepts only a string variable which is the path to where the image to be read is located, and the read image is returned as a Mat object. This method can be used as follows:

Mat matrix = imageCodecs.imread(Path to the image);

The following code describes how to do this:

```java
import org.opencv.core.Core;
import org.opencv.imgcodecs.Imgcodecs;
import org.opencv.core.Mat;
 public class WritingImages {
   public static void main(String args[]) {
     //Load the OpenCV core library

System.loadLibrary(Core.NATIVE_LIBRARY_NAME
);

     //Instantiate the imagecodecs class
     Imgcodecs imageCodecs = new Imgcodecs();

     //Read the Image from file then store it in a Matrix
object
     String file ="C:/USERS/OpenCV/image1.jpg";
     Mat matrix = imageCodecs.imread(file);

     System.out.println("Image has been Loaded");
     String file2 = "C:/USERS/OpenCV/image1_resaved.jpg";

     //Write the image
     imageCodecs.imwrite(file2, matrix);
     System.out.println("Image has been Saved");
   }
}
```

In this case, we have defined two string variables, "file" and 'file2." These have been used to specify the paths to our image, and they have then been passed to the imread() method. After running the program, open the specified path and you will find the image.

Chapter 5- Using Graphical User Interface

Now that you are aware of how to read and save images by use of the OpenCV Java library, it is possible to display the images in a separate window by the use of GUI libraries such as JavaFX and AWT/Swings.

Converting Mat to a Buffered Image

The imread() method is used for reading an image. The method reads an image and returns it in the form of a matrix. For us to be able to use this image with GUI libraries such as JavaFX and AWT/Swings, we have to convert the image into an object of the BufferedImage class which is of the java.awt.image.BufferedImage package.

The following steps should be followed for one to convert a Mat object of OpenCV into a BufferedImage object.

First, begin by encoding the Mat into a MatOfByte. This means that you convert the matrix into a matrix of byte. To do this, you should use the imencode() method which belongs to the ImageCodecs class. The method takes the following syntax:

imencode(ext, image, matOfByte);

The "ext" is a string parameter which specifies the format of the image, which can be either .jpg, .png, etc. the "image" parameter specifies the Mat object of the image. The parameter "matOfByte" represents an empty object of the class MatOfByte. The following code demonstrates how the image can be encoded:

//Read the image
Mat image = Imgcodecs.imread(file);

//instantiate an empty MatOfByte class
MatOfByte matOfByte = new MatOfByte();
//Convert the Mat object to a MatOfByte

Imgcodecs.imencode(".jpg", image, matOfByte);

Next the MatOfByte object should be converted to a byte array. The conversion can be done by use of the "toArray()" method. The method can be used as shown below:

byte[] byteArray = matOfByte.toArray();

You should then prepare the InputStream object. You just have to pass the byte array which was created previously to a constructor of the class "ByteArrayInputStream." This can be done as follows:

InputStream in = new ByteArrayInputStream(byteArray);

Next, you can prepare the InputStream object. The Input stream object created previously should be passed to the read() method of the ImageIO class. This will then give you a BufferredImage object. This is shown below:

BufferedImage bufImage = ImageIO.read(in);

Next, you can display the image in the GUI by use of an AWT/Swings frame. First, you have to read the image by use of the imread() method, and then follow the steps given previously so as to convert the image into a BufferedImage.

The JFrame class can then be instantiated and the Buffered image added to ContentPane of JFrame. This is shown below:

//Instantiate the JFrame
JFrame frame = new JFrame();

//Set the Content to JFrame
frame.getContentPane().add(new JLabel(new
ImageIcon(bufImage)));

frame.pack();

frame.setVisible(true);

You will then be done.

Consider the code given below which shows how you can read an image and then display it via a swing window by the use of the OpenCV library:

```
import java.awt.image.BufferedImage;
import java.io.InputStream;
import java.io.ByteArrayInputStream;
import javax.imageio.ImageIO;
import javax.swing.JFrame;
import javax.swing.ImageIcon;
import javax.swing.JLabel;
import org.opencv.core.Core;
import org.opencv.core.MatOfByte;
import org.opencv.core.Mat;
import org.opencv.imgcodecs.Imgcodecs;

public class DisplayingImagesUsingSwings {
  public static void main(String args[]) throws
Exception {
    //Load the OpenCV core library
    System.loadLibrary(
Core.NATIVE_LIBRARY_NAME );

    //Read the Image from file then store it in a Matrix
object
    String file = "C:/USERS/OpenCV/image1.jpg";
    Mat image = Imgcodecs.imread(file);

    //Encode the image
    MatOfByte matOfByte = new MatOfByte();
    Imgcodecs.imencode(".jpg", image, matOfByte);

    //Store the encoded Mat in byte array
    byte[] byteArray = matOfByte.toArray();
    //Prepare the Buffered Image
```

```
    InputStream in = new
ByteArrayInputStream(byteArray);
    BufferedImage bufImage = ImageIO.read(in);

    //Instantiate a JFrame
    JFrame frame = new JFrame();

    //Set Content to JFrame

    frame.getContentPane().add(new JLabel(new
ImageIcon(bufImage)));

    frame.pack();
    frame.setVisible(true);

    System.out.println("Image has been Loaded");
  }
}
```

Once you execute the above program, you should see the message that the image has been loaded. You will also see the image displayed on a window.

Using JavaFX

For you to display an image by use of JavaFX, first use imread() to read the image and then convert it into a BufferedImage. The BufferedImage should then be converted into a WritableImage by use of the syntax given below:

**WritableImage writableImage =
SwingFXUtils.toFXImage(bufImage, null);**

The WritableImage should then be passed to the constructor of the ImageView class as shown below:

**ImageView   imageView   =   new
ImageView(writableImage);**

The following is the complete code which can help you read an image and then display it via the JavaFX window by use of the OpenCV library. This is shown below:

```java
import java.awt.image.BufferedImage;

import java.io.IOException;
import java.io.ByteArrayInputStream;
import java.io.InputStream;

import javafx.application.Application;
import javafx.scene.Group;
import javafx.embed.swing.SwingFXUtils;
import javafx.scene.Scene;
import javafx.scene.image.WritableImage;
import javafx.scene.image.ImageView;
import javafx.stage.Stage;

import org.opencv.imgcodecs.Imgcodecs;
import javax.imageio.ImageIO;

import org.opencv.core.Mat;
import org.opencv.core.Core;
import org.opencv.core.MatOfByte;

public class DisplayingImagesJavaFX extends
Application {
  @Override
  public void start(Stage stage) throws IOException {
    WritableImage writableImage = loadImage();

    //Set the image view
    ImageView imageView = new
ImageView(writableImage);

    //Set the position of image
    imageView.setX(50);
    imageView.setY(25);
```

```java
//set the fit height and width of image view
imageView.setFitHeight(400);
imageView.setFitWidth(500);

//Set the preserve ratio of image view
imageView.setPreserveRatio(true);

//Create a Group object
Group root = new Group(imageView);

//Create a scene object
Scene scene = new Scene(root, 600, 400);

//Set the title to Stage
stage.setTitle("Loading an image");

//Add the scene to stage
stage.setScene(scene);

//Display contents of the stage
stage.show();
}
public WritableImage loadImage() throws
IOException {
//Load the OpenCV core library
System.loadLibrary(
Core.NATIVE_LIBRARY_NAME );

//Read the Image from file then store it in to
Matrix object
String file ="C:/USERS/OpenCV/image1.jpg";
Mat image = Imgcodecs.imread(file);

//Encode the image
MatOfByte matOfByte = new MatOfByte();
Imgcodecs.imencode(".jpg", image, matOfByte);

//Store the encoded Mat in byte array
byte[] byteArray = matOfByte.toArray();
```

```
   //Display the image
   InputStream in = new
ByteArrayInputStream(byteArray);
   BufferedImage bufImage = ImageIO.read(in);

   System.out.println("Image has been Loaded");

   WritableImage writableImage =
SwingFXUtils.toFXImage(bufImage, null);

   return writableImage;
  }
  public static void main(String args[]) {
   launch(args);
  }
}
```

After executing the program, you will be notified that the image has been loaded. The loaded image will also be displayed on a window.

Chapter 6- Converting Images

Images can be binary, BGR, grayscale, etc. With OpenCV, it is possible for you to convert an image from one form to another. The org.opencv.imgproc package provides the Imgproc class which can help one to convert an image from one color to another. Let us discuss how this can be done.

How to Convert Colored Images to Grayscale

For us to convert colored images into grayscale, we use the cvtColor() method. Below is the syntax for the method:

cvtColor(Mat src, Mat dst, int code)

The following takes three parameters as shown in the above syntax. The "src" parameter is a matrix which represents the source. The "dst" parameter is a matrix which represents the destination. The "code" parameter is an integer code which represents the conversion type, example, RGB to Grayscale.

For you to convert colored images into a grayscale, you have to pass the code Imgproc.COLOR_RGB2GRAY to the cvtColor() method together with the parameters for source and destination matrix.

In the code given below, we will be reading a colored image as a grayscale and then displaying it by use of the JavaFX window:

```
import java.awt.image.BufferedImage;
import org.opencv.core.Mat;
import org.opencv.core.Core;
import org.opencv.imgcodecs.Imgcodecs;
import org.opencv.imgproc.Imgproc;

import javafx.embed.swing.SwingFXUtils;
import javafx.scene.Scene;
import javafx.scene.Group;
```

```java
import javafx.scene.image.ImageView;
import javafx.application.Application;
import javafx.scene.image.WritableImage;

import javafx.stage.Stage;

public class ColorToGrayscale extends Application {
  @Override
  public void start(Stage stage) throws Exception {
    WritableImage writableImage =
loadAndConvert();

    // Set the image view
    ImageView imageView = new
ImageView(writableImage);

    // Set the position of image
    imageView.setX(10);
    imageView.setY(10);

    // set the fit height and width of image view
    imageView.setFitHeight(400);
    imageView.setFitWidth(600);

    // Set the preserve ratio of image view
    imageView.setPreserveRatio(true);

    // Create a Group object
    Group root = new Group(imageView);

    // Create a scene object
    Scene scene = new Scene(root, 600, 400);

    // Set the title to Stage
    stage.setTitle("Converting a colored image to
grayscale");

    // Add the scene to stage
    stage.setScene(scene);
```

```java
// Display the contents of stage
stage.show();
}
public WritableImage loadAndConvert() throws Exception {
//Load the OpenCV core library
System.loadLibrary( Core.NATIVE_LIBRARY_NAME );

String input = "C:/USERS/OpenCV/IMAGE1.jpg";

//Read the image
Mat src = Imgcodecs.imread(input);

//Create the empty destination matrix
Mat dst = new Mat();

//Convert the image to a gray sacle then save it in dst matrix
Imgproc.cvtColor(src, dst, Imgproc.COLOR_RGB2GRAY);

//Extract data from transformed image (dst)

byte[] data1 = new byte[dst.rows() * dst.cols() * (int)(dst.elemSize())];

dst.get(0, 0, data1);

//Create a Buffered image by use of the data

BufferedImage bufImage = new BufferedImage(dst.cols(),dst.rows(),

    BufferedImage.TYPE_BYTE_GRAY);

//Set the data elements to image
bufImage.getRaster().setDataElements(0, 0, dst.cols(), dst.rows(), data1);
```

```
   //Create a WritableImage

   WritableImage writableImage =
SwingFXUtils.toFXImage(bufImage, null);

   System.out.println("Converted to Grayscale");
   return writableImage;
 }
 public static void main(String args[]) throws
Exception {
   launch(args);
 }
}
```

You can run the program, and you will see your colored image displayed as a grayscale image.

How to Convert Colored Images to Binary

For us to convert a gray scale image into a binary image, we use the threshold() method. This method usually takes the syntax given below:

threshold(Mat src, Mat dst, double thresh, double maxval, int type)

As shown in the syntax, the method accepts five parameters. The "src" parameter is a Mat object which represents the input image. The "dst" parameter is a Mat object which represents the output image. The 'thresh" parameter is an integer which represents the threshold value. The "maxval" is an integer which represents the maximum value which is to be used with thresholding types for THRESH_BINARY and THRESH_BINARY_INV. The "type" parameter is an integer code which represents the type of conversion to be done, such as RGB to Grayscale.

For us to convert a gray scale image to binary, we have to pass the code Imgproc.THRESH_BINARY to the function together with the values for the other parameters.

In the example given below, we demonstrate one can read a colored image as binary and then display it by use of a JavaFX window:

```
import java.awt.image.BufferedImage;
import org.opencv.core.Mat;
import org.opencv.core.Core;
import org.opencv.imgcodecs.Imgcodecs;
import org.opencv.imgproc.Imgproc;
import javafx.embed.swing.SwingFXUtils;
import javafx.scene.Group;
import javafx.application.Application;
import javafx.scene.Scene;
import javafx.scene.image.WritableImage;
import javafx.scene.image.ImageView;
import javafx.stage.Stage;

public class ColorToBinary extends Application {
  @Override
  public void start(Stage stage) throws Exception {
    WritableImage writableImage =
loadAndConvert();

    // Set the image view
    ImageView imageView = new
ImageView(writableImage);

    // Set the position of image
    imageView.setX(10);
    imageView.setY(10);

    // set the fit height and the width of image view
    imageView.setFitHeight(400);
    imageView.setFitWidth(600);

    // Set the preserve ratio of image view
```

```
    imageView.setPreserveRatio(true);

    // Create a Group object
    Group root = new Group(imageView);

    // Create a scene object
    Scene scene = new Scene(root, 600, 400);

    // Set the title to Stage
    stage.setTitle("Loading the image");

    // Add the scene to stage
    stage.setScene(scene);

    // Display the contents of stage
    stage.show();
  }
  public WritableImage loadAndConvert() throws
Exception {
    // Load the OpenCV core library
    System.loadLibrary(
Core.NATIVE_LIBRARY_NAME );

    // Instantiate the Imgcodecs class
    Imgcodecs imageCodecs = new Imgcodecs();

    // File input = new
File("C:/USERS/OpenCV/image1.jpg");
    String input = "C:/USERS/OpenCV/image1.jpg";

    // Read the image
    Mat src = imageCodecs.imread(input);

    // Create the destination matrix
    Mat dst = new Mat();

    // Convert to binary image...
```

```java
    Imgproc.threshold(src, dst, 200, 500,
Imgproc.THRESH_BINARY);

    // Extract the data from transformed image (dst)

    byte[] data1 = new byte[dst.rows() * dst.cols() *
(int)(dst.elemSize())];

    dst.get(0, 0, data1);

    // Create a Buffered image using data

    BufferedImage bufImage = new
BufferedImage(dst.cols(),dst.rows(),

      BufferedImage.TYPE_BYTE_GRAY);

    // Set the data elements to image

    bufImage.getRaster().setDataElements(0, 0,
dst.cols(), dst.rows(), data1);

    // Create a Writable image

    WritableImage writableImage =
SwingFXUtils.toFXImage(bufImage, null);

    System.out.println("Converted to binary");
    return writableImage;
  }
  public static void main(String args[]) throws
Exception {
    launch(args);
  }
}
```

You can then run the program, and you will see the changes made to the image you specify.

```java
    imageView.setPreserveRatio(true);

    // Create a Group object
    Group root = new Group(imageView);

    // Create a scene object
    Scene scene = new Scene(root, 600, 400);

    // Set the title to Stage
    stage.setTitle("Loading the image");

    // Add the scene to stage
    stage.setScene(scene);

    // Display the contents of stage
    stage.show();
  }
  public WritableImage loadAndConvert() throws
Exception {
    // Load the OpenCV core library
    System.loadLibrary(
Core.NATIVE_LIBRARY_NAME );

    // Instantiate the Imgcodecs class
    Imgcodecs imageCodecs = new Imgcodecs();

    // File input = new
File("C:/USERS/OpenCV/image1.jpg");
    String input = "C:/USERS/OpenCV/image1.jpg";

    // Read the image
    Mat src = imageCodecs.imread(input);

    // Create the destination matrix
    Mat dst = new Mat();

    // Convert to binary image...
```

```
Imgproc.threshold(src, dst, 200, 500,
Imgproc.THRESH_BINARY);

// Extract the data from transformed image (dst)

byte[] data1 = new byte[dst.rows() * dst.cols() *
(int)(dst.elemSize())];

dst.get(0, 0, data1);

// Create a Buffered image using data

BufferedImage bufImage = new
BufferedImage(dst.cols(),dst.rows(),

   BufferedImage.TYPE_BYTE_GRAY);

// Set the data elements to image

bufImage.getRaster().setDataElements(0, 0,
dst.cols(), dst.rows(), data1);

// Create a Writable image

WritableImage writableImage =
SwingFXUtils.toFXImage(bufImage, null);

System.out.println("Converted to binary");
return writableImage;
  }
  public static void main(String args[]) throws
Exception {
    launch(args);
  }
}
```

You can then run the program, and you will see the changes made to the image you specify.

How to convert a Grayscale Image to Binary

The steps discussed previously can help you convert your grayscale image to binary. You just have to pass the path where your grayscale image is located and it will be converted to binary. The following Java code demonstrates this. In the code, a grayscale image will be read as binary, and it will then be displayed by use of a JavaFX window:

```java
import java.awt.image.BufferedImage;
import org.opencv.core.Mat;
import org.opencv.core.Core;
import org.opencv.imgcodecs.Imgcodecs;
import javafx.application.Application;
import org.opencv.imgproc.Imgproc;
import javafx.embed.swing.SwingFXUtils;
import javafx.scene.Scene;
import javafx.scene.Group;
import javafx.scene.image.ImageView;
import javafx.stage.Stage;
import javafx.scene.image.WritableImage;

public class GrayScaleToBinary extends Application {
  @Override
  public void start(Stage stage) throws Exception {
    WritableImage writableImage =
loadAndConvert();

    // Set the image view
    ImageView imageView = new
ImageView(writableImage);

    // Set the position of image
    imageView.setX(10);
    imageView.setY(10);

    // Set fit height and the width of image view
    imageView.setFitHeight(400);
```

```
        imageView.setFitWidth(600);

        // Set the preserve ratio of image view
        imageView.setPreserveRatio(true);

        // Create a Group object
        Group root = new Group(imageView);

        // Create a scene object
        Scene scene = new Scene(root, 600, 400);

        // Set the title to Stage
        stage.setTitle("Converting grayscale to binary image");

        // Add scene to stage
        stage.setScene(scene);

        // Display the contents of stage
        stage.show();
    }
    public WritableImage loadAndConvert() throws
Exception {
        // Load the OpenCV core library
        System.loadLibrary(
Core.NATIVE_LIBRARY_NAME );

        // Instantiate the imagecodecs class
        Imgcodecs imageCodecs = new Imgcodecs();

        String input = "E:/OpenCV/images/grayscale.jpg";

        // Read the image
        Mat src = imageCodecs.imread(input);

        // Create the destination matrix
        Mat dst = new Mat();

        // Convert to binary image
```

```java
    Imgproc.threshold(src, dst, 200, 500,
Imgproc.THRESH_BINARY);

    // Extract data from transformed image (dst)

    byte[] data1 = new byte[dst.rows() * dst.cols() *
(int)(dst.elemSize())];

    dst.get(0, 0, data1);

    // Create a Buffered image from the data

    BufferedImage bufImage = new
BufferedImage(dst.cols(),dst.rows(),

      BufferedImage.TYPE_BYTE_BINARY);

    // Set the data elements to image

    bufImage.getRaster().setDataElements(0, 0,
dst.cols(), dst.rows(), data1);

    // Create a Writable image

    WritableImage writableImage =
SwingFXUtils.toFXImage(bufImage, null);

    System.out.println("Conversion to binary done");
    return writableImage;
  }
  public static void main(String args[]) throws
Exception {
    launch(args);
  }
}
```

You can then run the program and observe the changes to the images you have specified.

Changing ColorSpaces in Python

For us to convert image colors in Python with OpenCV, we use the "cv2.cvtColor(input_image, flag)" method. The flag denotes the type of conversion which is to be done. To convert from BGR to Gray, we use the cv2.COLOR_BGR2GRAY flag. To convert from BGR to HSV, we use the flag. If you need to know the other types of flags which can be used, just run the following command on your Python terminal:

```
>>> import cv2
>>> flags = [i for i in dir(cv2) if i.startswith('COLOR_')]
>>> print flags
```

In HSV, it becomes easy for one to represent a color space. We will be trying to extract an object with a blue color. The following are the necessary steps for you to do this;

- Take every frame of video
- Convert BGR to the HSV color-space
- Threshold the HSV image for the range of the blue color
- Extract only the blue object

The code for this is given below:

```
import cv2
import numpy as np

cap = cv2.VideoCapture(0)

while(1):

    # Take every frame
    _, frame = cap.read()
    # Convert the BGR to HSV
    hsv = cv2.cvtColor(frame, cv2.COLOR_BGR2HSV)
```

```python
# define a range of the blue color in HSV
lower_blue = np.array([110,50,50])
upper_blue = np.array([130,255,255])

# Threshold HSV image to obtain only blue colors
mask = cv2.inRange(hsv, lower_green, upper_green)

# Bitwise-AND mask the original image
res = cv2.bitwise_and(frame,frame, mask= mask)

cv2.imshow('frame',frame)
cv2.imshow('mask',mask)
cv2.imshow('res',res)
k = cv2.waitKey(5) & 0xFF
if k == 27:
    break

cv2.destroyAllWindows()
```

You can then run the program and observe the original image, the masked image, and the final result.

Chapter 7- OpenCV and the Camera

You can use OpenCV so as to capture frames by use of the system camera. The class named VideoCapture provided in the org.opencv.videoio package comes with methods which can be used to capture videos by use of the camera. Let us discuss how this can be done in a step-by-step manner:

The first step should involve the loading of the OpenCV native library. As usual, this will be done by use of the loadLibrary() function. This is shown below:

System.loadLibrary(Core.NATIVE_LIBRARY_NAME);

Create an instance of the video capture class. This can be done as follows:
VideoCapture capture = new VideoCapture(0);

The read() method provided in the VideoCapture class can then help you to read the frames from the camera. The method usually accepts an object of Mat class which will be storing the frame read. This is shown below:

Mat matrix = new Mat();
capture.read(matrix);

In the code given below, we will be capturing an frame from the camera and this frame will be displayed by use of a JavaFX window. The captured frame will also be saved. Here is the code:

import java.awt.image.DataBufferByte;
import java.awt.image.BufferedImage;
import java.awt.image.WritableRaster;

import java.io.IOException;
import java.io.FileNotFoundException;

```java
import javafx.application.Application;
import javafx.scene.Group;
import javafx.embed.swing.SwingFXUtils;
import javafx.scene.Scene;
import javafx.scene.image.WritableImage;
import javafx.scene.image.ImageView;
import javafx.stage.Stage;

import org.opencv.core.Core;
import org.opencv.imgcodecs.Imgcodecs;
import org.opencv.core.Mat;
import org.opencv.videoio.VideoCapture;

public class CameraFrameJavaFX  extends
Application {
  Mat matrix = null;

  @Override

  public void start(Stage stage) throws
FileNotFoundException, IOException {

    // Capture the snapshot from camera
    CameraFrameJavaFX  obj = new
CameraFrameJavaFX ();
    WritableImage writableImage =
obj.capureSnapShot();

    // Save the image
    obj.saveImage();

    // Set the image view
    ImageView imageView = new
ImageView(writableImage);

    // set the fit height and width of image view
    imageView.setFitHeight(400);
    imageView.setFitWidth(600);
```

```java
    // Set the preserve ratio of image view
    imageView.setPreserveRatio(true);

    // Create a Group object
    Group root = new Group(imageView);

    // Create a scene object
    Scene scene = new Scene(root, 600, 400);

    // Set the title to Stage
    stage.setTitle("Capturing an image");

    // Add a scene to stage
    stage.setScene(scene);

    // Display the contents of stage
    stage.show();
}
    public WritableImage capureSnapShot() {
    WritableImage WritableImage = null;

    // Load the OpenCV core library
    System.loadLibrary(
Core.NATIVE_LIBRARY_NAME );

    // Instantiate the VideoCapture class (camera:: 0)
    VideoCapture capture = new VideoCapture(0);

    // Read the next video frame from camera
    Mat matrix = new Mat();
    capture.read(matrix);

    // If the camera is opened
    if( capture.isOpened()) {
        // If there is a next video frame
        if (capture.read(matrix)) {
            // Create a BuffredImage from matrix
            BufferedImage image = new
BufferedImage(matrix.width(),
```

```
          matrix.height(),
BufferedImage.TYPE_3BYTE_BGR);

      WritableRaster raster = image.getRaster();

      DataBufferByte dataBuffer = (DataBufferByte)
raster.getDataBuffer();

      byte[] data = dataBuffer.getData();
      matrix.get(0, 0, data);
      this.matrix = matrix;

      // Create the Writable Image
      WritableImage =
SwingFXUtils.toFXImage(image, null);
     }
   }
   return WritableImage;
 }
 public void saveImage() {
   // Save the Image
   String file = "C:/OpenCV/images/sanpshot.jpg";

   // Instantiate the imgcodecs class
   Imgcodecs imageCodecs = new Imgcodecs();

   // Save it again
   imageCodecs.imwrite(file, matrix);
 }
 public static void main(String args[]) {
   launch(args);
 }
}
```

You will observe that the captured image will be displayed on a
window. Navigate to the path you have specified in the code,
and you will find that the image has been saved there.

Detecting Faces in a Picture

You can detect faces which are in a picture using OpenCV. First, begin by loading the OpenCV native library by calling the loadLibrary() function as shown below:

System.loadLibrary(Core.NATIVE_LIBRARY_NAME);

Next, create an instance of the CascadeClassifier class which is provided by the borg.opencv.objdetect package. This will help in loading the classifier file. To instantiate the class, pass the lbpcascade_frontalface.xml, which is an xml file as shown below:

String xmlFile = "E:/OpenCV/facedetect/lbpcascade_frontalface.xml";

CascadeClassifier classifier = new CascadeClassifier(xmlFile);

You can then detect the faces contained in the picture by use of the detectMultiScale() method of the CascadeClassifier class. The method accepts Mat object which holds the input image and an object of MatOfRect class for storing the detected faces. This is shown below:

MatOfRect faceDetections = new MatOfRect();
classifier.detectMultiScale(src, faceDetections);

The following is the complete code which shows how this can be done:

import org.opencv.core.Core;
import org.opencv.core.MatOfRect;
import org.opencv.core.Mat;
import org.opencv.core.Point;

```java
import org.opencv.core.Scalar;
import org.opencv.core.Rect;

import org.opencv.imgproc.Imgproc;
import org.opencv.imgcodecs.Imgcodecs;
import org.opencv.objdetect.CascadeClassifier;

public class FaceDetection {
  public static void main (String[] args) {
    // Load the OpenCV core library
    System.loadLibrary(
Core.NATIVE_LIBRARY_NAME );

    // Read the Image from file and store it in a Matrix
object
    String file ="E:/OpenCV/images/photo.jpg";
    Mat src = Imgcodecs.imread(file);

    // Instantiate the CascadeClassifier
    String xmlFile =
"E:/OpenCV/facedetect/lbpcascade_frontalface.xml";
    CascadeClassifier classifier = new
CascadeClassifier(xmlFile);

    // Detect the face in the photo
    MatOfRect faceDetections = new MatOfRect();
    classifier.detectMultiScale(src, faceDetections);
    System.out.println(String.format("Detected %s
faces",
        faceDetections.toArray().length));

    // Draw the boxes
    for (Rect rect : faceDetections.toArray()) {
      Imgproc.rectangle(
        src,              // where should draw the box
        new Point(rect.x, rect.y),          // bottom left
        new Point(rect.x + rect.width, rect.y +
rect.height), // top right
        new Scalar(0, 0, 255),
```

```
        3                              // RGB colour
    );
}
```

// Write the image

```
Imgcodecs.imwrite("E:/OpenCV/images/photo2.jpg",
src);

    System.out.println("Image has been Processed");
    }
}
```

Run the program and open the file saved in the path you have specified. You will find that the faces in your image have been identified and a rectangle has been drawn on each face.

Rather than detecting faces on a picture, with OpenCV, you can detect a face by use of the camera. Once the face has been detected, you can display it by use of the JavaFX window. The following Java code demonstrates how this can be done:

```java
import java.awt.image.DataBufferByte;
import java.awt.image.BufferedImage;
import java.awt.image.WritableRaster;

import java.io.IOException;

import javafx.application.Application;
import java.io.FileNotFoundException;
import javafx.scene.Group;
import javafx.scene.Scene;
import javafx.scene.image.ImageView;
import javafx.scene.image.WritableImage;
import javafx.stage.Stage;
import org.opencv.core.Core;
import org.opencv.core.MatOfRect;
import org.opencv.core.Mat;
```

```java
import org.opencv.core.Point;
import org.opencv.core.Scalar;
import org.opencv.core.Rect;
import org.opencv.imgcodecs.Imgcodecs;
import org.opencv.objdetect.CascadeClassifier;
import org.opencv.imgproc.Imgproc;
import org.opencv.videoio.VideoCapture;

public class FaceDetection extends Application {
  Mat matrix = null;

  @Override

  public void start(Stage stage) throws
FileNotFoundException, IOException {

    // Capture the snapshot from camera
    FaceDetection obj = new FaceDetection();
    WritableImage writableImage =
obj.capureFrame();

    // Save the image
    obj.saveImage();

    // Set the image view
    ImageView imageView = new
ImageView(writableImage);

    // set the fit height and the width of image view
    imageView.setFitHeight(400);
    imageView.setFitWidth(600);

    // Set the preserve ratio of image view
    imageView.setPreserveRatio(true);

    // Create a Group object
    Group root = new Group(imageView);

    // Create a scene object
```

```java
        Scene scene = new Scene(root, 600, 400);

        // Set the title to Stage
        stage.setTitle("Capturing the image");

        // Add scene to stage
        stage.setScene(scene);

        // Display the contents of stage
        stage.show();
    }
    public WritableImage capureFrame() {
        WritableImage writableImage = null;

        // Load the OpenCV core library
        System.loadLibrary(
Core.NATIVE_LIBRARY_NAME );

        // Instantiate the VideoCapture class (camera:: 0)
        VideoCapture capture = new VideoCapture(0);

        // Read the next video frame from camera
        Mat matrix = new Mat();
        capture.read(matrix);

        // If the camera is opened
        if(!capture.isOpened()) {
            System.out.println("camera has not been
detected");
        } else
            System.out.println("Camera has been detected
");

        // If there is a next video frame
        if (capture.read(matrix)) {
            String file =
"E:/OpenCV/facedetect/lbpcascade_frontalface.xml";
            CascadeClassifier classifier = new
CascadeClassifier(file);
```

```java
MatOfRect faceDetections = new MatOfRect();
classifier.detectMultiScale(matrix, faceDetections);
System.out.println(String.format("Detected %s faces",
    faceDetections.toArray().length));

// Draw the boxes
for (Rect rect : faceDetections.toArray()) {
  Imgproc.rectangle(
    matrix,                          //where the box to be drawn
    new Point(rect.x, rect.y),       //bottom left
    new Point(rect.x + rect.width, rect.y + rect.height),//top right
    new Scalar(0, 0, 255)            //RGB color
  );
}
// Creating BuffredImage from the matrix

BufferedImage image = new BufferedImage(matrix.width(), matrix.height(),

  BufferedImage.TYPE_3BYTE_BGR);

WritableRaster raster = image.getRaster();
DataBufferByte dataBuffer = (DataBufferByte) raster.getDataBuffer();
byte[] data = dataBuffer.getData();
matrix.get(0, 0, data);

this.matrix = matrix;

// Create the Writable Image
writableImage = SwingFXUtils.toFXImage(image, null);
}
return writableImage;
```

```
}
public void saveImage() {
  // Save the Image
  String file = "E:/OpenCV/images/face.jpg";

  // Instantiating the imagecodecs class
  Imgcodecs imageCodecs = new Imgcodecs();

  // Save it again
  imageCodecs.imwrite(file, matrix);
}
public static void main(String args[]) {
  launch(args);
}
}
```

Run the program and allow the camera to take a photo of you. You will see a rectangle drawn on your face, meaning that the face has been detected.

Chapter 8- Geometric Transformations of Images

In Python, OpenCV comes with two functions for transformations, cv2.warpAffine and cv2.warpPerspective, which can be used for all types of transformations. The cv2.warpAffine takes a transformation of 2*3, while the cv2.warpPerspective takes a 3*3 transformation as the input.

Scaling

This is the process of resizing an image. The function cv2.resize() of OpenCV helps us scale images. You can specify the size that you want for the image, or specify the scaling factor. There is also different interpolation methods, with the common ones being cv2.INTER_AREA used for shrinking and cv2.INTER_CUBIC (slow) and cv2.INTER_LINEAR used for zooming. By default, the cv2.INTER_LINEAR interpolation method is used for the purpose of resizing images. The following are the methods which can help you to resize an input image:

import cv2
import numpy as np

img = cv2.imread(**'img.jpg'**)

res = cv2.resize(img,**None**,fx=**2**, fy=**2**, interpolation = cv2.INTER_CUBIC**)**

#OR

height, width = img.shape[**:2**]
res = cv2.resize(img,(**2***width, **2***height), interpolation = cv2.INTER_CUBIC**)**

In the first method, we specified the scaling factor for both the x and the y axis. The interpolation method has also been specified. In the second method, we have doubled the size of the image manually by multiplying the width and the height by 2.

Translation

This is just changing the position or location of an object. If you need to shift the image in an (x,y) direction, you can create a transformation matrix. The matrix can then be converted into a numpy array of np.float32 type and then pass it to the cv2.warpAffine() function. Consider the example given below:

```
import cv2
import numpy as np

img = cv2.imread('Pic1.jpg',0)
rows,cols = img.shape

M = np.float32([[1,0,100],[0,1,50]])
dst = cv2.warpAffine(img,M,(cols,rows))

cv2.imshow('img',dst)
cv2.waitKey(0)
cv2.destroyAllWindows()
```

The code shows a shift of (100,50).

Rotation

This is changing the position of an image by an angle. OpenCV has a scaled rotation with a center for transformation which can be changed so that you can rotate the image to any location that you prefer. The cv2.getRotationMatrix2D method of OpenCV is normally used for transformation purposes. Consider the example given below:

```
img = cv2.imread('Pic1.jpg',0)
rows,cols = img.shape
M = cv2.getRotationMatrix2D((cols/2,rows/2),90,1)
dst = cv2.warpAffine(img,M,(cols,rows))
```

The above code rotates the image at an angle of 90 degrees with no scaling with respect to the center.

Affine Transformation

This is a type of transformation in which all the parallel lines in the image remains to be parallel in the transformed image. For the transformation matrix to be obtained, three points for the input image and three points for the output image are needed. The function cv2.getAffineTransform of OpenCV creates a 2*3 matrix which is then passed to the cv2.warpAffine method. The following Python code demonstrates this:

```
img = cv2.imread('draw.png')
rows,cols,ch = img.shape

pts1 = np.float32([[50,50],[200,50],[50,200]])
pts2 = np.float32([[10,100],[200,50],[100,250]])

M = cv2.getAffineTransform(pts1,pts2)

dst = cv2.warpAffine(img,M,(cols,rows))

plt.subplot(121),plt.imshow(img),plt.title('Input')
plt.subplot(122),plt.imshow(dst),plt.title('Output')
plt.show()
```

In Java, the imgproc class provides the warpAffine() method which can be used for affine transformation. The method takes the syntax given below:

Imgproc.warpAffine(src, dst, tranformMatrix, size);

The first two arguments are obvious. The transformMatrix parameter describes the transformation matrix, while the size parameter is the size of the output image. The following code demonstrates how you can perform affine transformation on an image in Java:

```
import org.opencv.core.Core;
import org.opencv.core.MatOfPoint2f;
import org.opencv.core.Mat;
import org.opencv.core.Point;
import org.opencv.imgcodecs.Imgcodecs;
import org.opencv.core.Size;
import org.opencv.imgproc.Imgproc;

public class AffineTranslation {
  public static void main(String args[]) {
    // Load the OpenCV core library
    System.loadLibrary( Core.NATIVE_LIBRARY_NAME );

    // Read the Image from file and store it in a Matrix object
    String file ="E:/OpenCV/images/input.jpg";
    Mat src = Imgcodecs.imread(file);

    //Create an empty matrix for storing the result
    Mat dst = new Mat();

    Point p1 = new Point( 0,0 );
    Point p2 = new Point( src.cols() - 1, 0 );
    Point p3 = new Point( 0, src.rows() - 1 );
    Point p4 = new Point( src.cols()*0.0, src.rows()*0.33 );
    Point p5 = new Point( src.cols()*0.85, src.rows()*0.25 );
    Point p6 = new Point( src.cols()*0.15, src.rows()*0.7 );

    MatOfPoint2f ma1 = new MatOfPoint2f(p1,p2,p3);
    MatOfPoint2f ma2 = new MatOfPoint2f(p4,p5,p6);

    // Create the transformation matrix
```

```java
    Mat tranformMatrix =
Imgproc.getAffineTransform(ma1,ma2);

    // Create an object of class Size
    Size size = new Size(src.cols(), src.cols());

    // Apply Wrap Affine
    Imgproc.warpAffine(src, dst, tranformMatrix,
size);

    // Write the image


Imgcodecs.imwrite("E:/OpenCV/images/Affinetranslate.jp
g", dst);

    System.out.println("Image has been Processed");
  }
}
```

You can then run the program, and you will get the message that the image has been processed. Navigate to the path you have specified, and open the new image named Affinetranslate.jpg. You will see that some changes have been made to the image.

Chapter 9- Video Analysis

Meanshift

Suppose you have a set of points such as a distribution of pixels. You have a small window which you want to move to the position with maximum pixel density. It is a good application of meanshift.

For us to implement meanshift in OpenCV and Python, we should first setup the target, and identify its histogram so as to backproject the target on every frame for calculation of the meanshift. The window's initial location should also be provided. In the case of histogram, only Hue will be considered. False values should be avoided for the purpose of low light. The cv2.inRange() function can be used for the purpose of discarding the low light values. This is demonstrated below:

```
import numpy as np
import cv2

cap = cv2.VideoCapture('video1.flv')

# take the first frame of video
ret,frame = cap.read()

# setup the initial location of the window
r,h,c,w = 250,90,400,125  # hardcoded values
track_window = (c,r,w,h)

# set up ROI for tracking
roi = frame[r:r+h, c:c+w]
hsv_roi = cv2.cvtColor(roi, cv2.COLOR_BGR2HSV)

mask = cv2.inRange(hsv_roi, np.array((0., 60.,32.)),
np.array((180.,255.,255.)))
```

```
roi_hist =
cv2.calcHist([hsv_roi],[0],mask,[180],[0,180])
cv2.normalize(roi_hist,roi_hist,0,255,cv2.NORM_MI
NMAX)

# Setup the termination criteria, either 10 iteration or
move by atleast 1 pt

term_crit = ( cv2.TERM_CRITERIA_EPS |
cv2.TERM_CRITERIA_COUNT, 10, 1 )

while(1):
  ret ,frame = cap.read()

  if ret == True:
    hsv = cv2.cvtColor(frame,
cv2.COLOR_BGR2HSV)
    dst =
cv2.calcBackProject([hsv],[0],roi_hist,[0,180],1)

    # apply the meanshift to obtain the new location

    ret, track_window = cv2.meanShift(dst,
track_window, term_crit)

    # Draw it on the image
    x,y,w,h = track_window
    img2 = cv2.rectangle(frame, (x,y), (x+w,y+h),
255,2)
    cv2.imshow('img2',img2)

    k = cv2.waitKey(60) & 0xff
    if k == 27:
      break
    else:
      cv2.imwrite(chr(k)+".jpg",img2)

  else:
    break
```

```
cv2.destroyAllWindows()
cap.release()
```

Camshift

This brings about a mechanism to play around with the size of the window. It first begins with the meanshift, then the window size is changed by use of a formula. The calculation of the best fitting ellipse is also determined. Meanshift is then applied with a new scaled search window and the previous window location. This process is continued until one gets the accuracy which is needed. Camshift is similar to meanshift in OpenCV, with the difference being that it returns a rotated rectangle and the box parameters which are used for passing as a search window in the next iteration. The following code demonstrates this:

```
import numpy as np
import cv2

cap = cv2.VideoCapture('video1.flv')

# take the first frame of your video
ret,frame = cap.read()

# setup the window's initial location
r,h,c,w = 250,90,400,125  # hardcoded values
track_window = (c,r,w,h)

# set up ROI for tracking
roi = frame[r:r+h, c:c+w]
hsv_roi = cv2.cvtColor(roi, cv2.COLOR_BGR2HSV)
mask = cv2.inRange(hsv_roi, np.array((0., 60.,32.)),
np.array((180.,255.,255.)))
roi_hist =
cv2.calcHist([hsv_roi],[0],mask,[180],[0,180])
cv2.normalize(roi_hist,roi_hist,0,255,cv2.NORM_MI
NMAX)
```

```python
# Setup termination criteria, either to 10 iteration or
move by at least 1 pt
term_crit = ( cv2.TERM_CRITERIA_EPS |
cv2.TERM_CRITERIA_COUNT, 10, 1 )

while(1):
    ret ,frame = cap.read()

    if ret == True:
        hsv = cv2.cvtColor(frame,
cv2.COLOR_BGR2HSV)
        dst =
cv2.calcBackProject([hsv],[0],roi_hist,[0,180],1)

        # apply meanshift to get the new location
        ret, track_window = cv2.CamShift(dst,
track_window, term_crit)

        # Draw it on the image
        pts = cv2.boxPoints(ret)
        pts = np.int0(pts)
        img2 = cv2.polylines(frame,[pts],True, 255,2)
        cv2.imshow('img2',img2)

        k = cv2.waitKey(60) & 0xff
        if k == 27:
            break
        else:
            cv2.imwrite(chr(k)+".jpg",img2)

    else:
        break

cv2.destroyAllWindows()
cap.release()
```

You will see changes in the frames.

Conclusion

We have come to the end of this book. OpenCV is a computer vision library compatible with Java, C, C++, and Python. It is commonly used in image and video processing. If there is a need for such features in your application, this is a good library for you to use. You can even use the library with the camera of your computer to take pictures and videos and then analyze them for any parts and objects you need to detect. It is a widely applicable computer library in today's software applications.

www.ingramcontent.com/pod-product-compliance
Lightning Source LLC
Chambersburg PA
CBHW070859070326
40690CB00009B/1915

www.ingramcontent.com/pod-product-compliance
Lightning Source LLC
Chambersburg PA
CBHW070859070326
40690CB00009B/1915